BROOME

Today Broome is a booming tourist town with a unique culture and history that attracts visitors from all over the world to experience paradise in an ideal climate on the edge of the pristine Kimberley wilderness.

Broome owes it's existence to the worlds largest species of pearl oyster discovered in Roebuck Bay in 1861. It was established as a pearling port in the 1880's and quickly became populated by people of many nationalities such as Europeans, Japanese, Chinese, Malays, and others in search of their fortune from the pearling industry. Along with the local Australian indigenous people this cultural melting pot created the distinctive character and charm of the town today.

Pearling still remains a thriving industry with Broome producing many of the world's finest pearls. Times were tough in the early days with hundreds of divers losing their lives due to the bends and other dangers of the sea. Later, the advent of plastics in the 1950's threatened the industry that was dependent greatly on pearl shell for producing buttons. The technological leap of culturing pearls revitalised the industry where shell is mostly a by-product.

Today Broome caters well for tourists with a wide variety of accommodation, dining, tours and activities to suit a range of budgets. Broome is also a gateway to the 400,000 square kilometre Kimberley region that is considered to be one of the last frontiers in the world.

The Dampier Peninsula north of Broome is a relatively close Kimberley destination mostly consisting of Aboriginal land that is also rich in pearling history. Many communities and outstations have embraced tourism sharing their culture and amazing wilderness.

The area has a seemingly endless unspoiled coastline, tranquil community settings and relaxing holiday retreats with pristine clear waters offering the chance to swim, snorkel and fish. The way the peculiar red cliffs contrast against clean white sand beaches and turquoise blue waters intrigues many.

Broome and beyond is a great Australian holiday experience for those who just want to simply relax, and for those who are more adventurous. For more information on tours, activities and accommodation contact:

Broome Visitor Centre: Ph: 1800 883 777   www.ebroome.com/tourism

Streeters Jetty

Historic original Broome town centre

Cable Beach

Gantheaume Point

Cable Beach Camels

Anastasia's Pool - Built by a former lighthouse keeper for his arthritic wife - Gantheaume Point

Gantheaume Point

The Broome Crocodile Park was established in 1983 by Malcom Douglas as a research centre and allows the general public to get a safe close look and understanding of these ancient reptiles. Malcom is well known throughout Australia and the world for his TV adventure films.

In recent years the crocodile park has become so popular that Malcom is expanding it to 30ha block 16km from town on the Main highway. Malcom also has a commercial crocodile farm and is working within the Crocodile Specialist Group to ensure the survival of endangered species around the world. Ph: (08) 9192 1489

Malcom Douglas at his crocodile park

Broome Crocodile Park

Broome Jetty

Roger Colless from Spirit of Broome Hovercraft tours at the Dinosaur footprints - Roebuck Bay

Flying along smoothly on a cushion of air on the 'Spirit of Broome' hovercraft is a highlight for countless Broome visitors. This amphibious craft allows access to many places normally inaccessible to boat or drive tours.

A range of flights are available to suit most budgets depending on the tides and availability. Some of these include: sunset cocktail flights, breakfast, deluxe breakfast, and recently a 3 hour silver service dinner flight.

Flights depart everyday except in February from the picturesque base near the Broome deep water port and jetty

The hovercraft base also features dinghy hire, Anchors Tea Garden and Function Centre, and the 'Port of Pearls' Art Gallery.   www.broomehovercraft.com   Ph: (08) 9193 5025

WW2 Dornier Flying Boat wrecks bombed by Japanese zeros March 3, 1942

Spirit of Broome Hovercraft Base (also Anchors Tea Garden) - Roebuck Bay

Willie Creek Pearl Farm

Willie Creek Pearl Farm

Stuart Howe with his Microlight

Airborne Adventures offers the public the chance to be a pilot for a day over the spectacular scenery of Broome. Unlike most aircraft you can feel the air in your face and have a bird's eye view from the open cockpit.

Stuart Howe has 27 years experience in sport aviation and is also a licenced aircraft engineer. Departing from the General Aviation Terminal on the northern side of the Broome international Airport, Stuart operates flights at sunrise and sunset.
Ph: 0409 996 090

Cable Beach

Cable Beach

Statues of the pioneers of the cultured pearl industry

Broome Pearl Diver Statue

Japanese Cemetery - The final resting place for over 900 Japanese pearl divers

Experience over 140 years of Broome's unique history back through the life and times of the pearl divers and view two of the last surviving perfectly restored pearl luggers. Former pearl diver 'Salty Dog' brings the past to life in his captivating stories. His exciting guided tours cover an array of pearling equipment, with memorabilia from actual hard hat diving suits to the hand-powered pumps which fed precious air to the divers below.... A very interesting tour by an enthralling character that is not easily forgotten. Ph: (08) 9192 2059

Pearling master Richard (Salty Dog) Baillieu at the Pearl Luggers Museum - Chinatown

Shinju Matsuri - Japanese, meaning 'Festival of the Pearl' This exciting event is a vivid display of cultural dress, art, food, music and dance. It was Originally set around the August full moon between August 15th and 22nd in 1970 to combine the various cultural festivals (but with a commercial element) to encourage community spirit and to keep alive the romance of the pearling industry. In recent years organisers have endeavoured to return to the original concept of the festival whilst making it relevant to Broome today and it's many businesses.

Shinju Matsuri Festival held August / September

Sun Pictures - The worlds oldest operating outdoor picture theatre est. 1916

Cable Beach Sunburst

Broome in the wet season

Afternoon wet season rain near Town Beach

Kooljamin at Cape Leveque

Cape Leveque

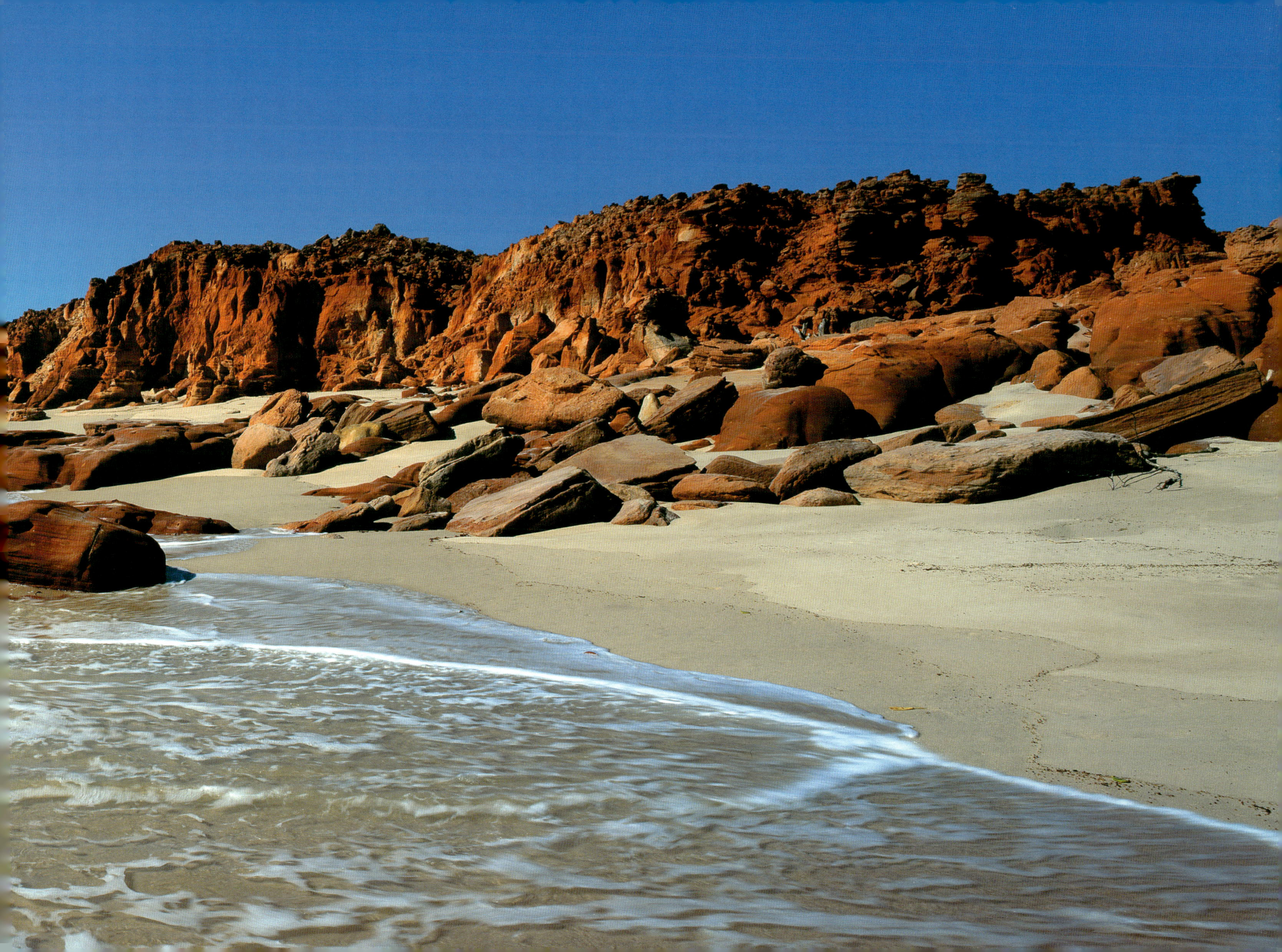

Cape Leveque

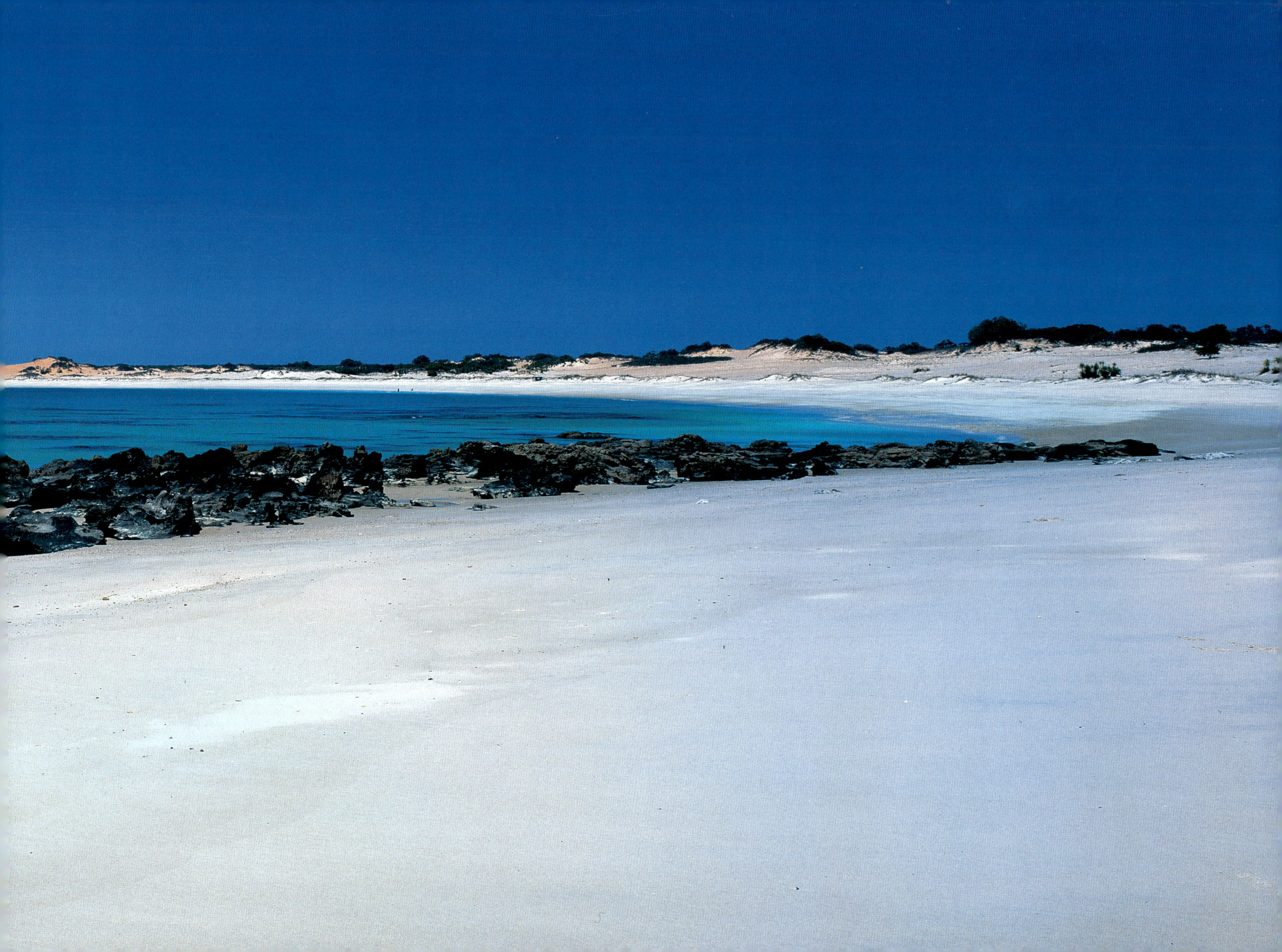

Cape Leveque sunrise

Cape Leveque red cliffs

Another magical Cable Beach sunset